Presented to

Lucille Anne D. Capul

From

Family

Date

Jan 13, 1998

Children's Bible Dictionary

Children's Bible Dictionary

Text by

Debbie Butcher

Illustrations by

Samuel J. Butcher

BAKER
A DIVISION OF
Baker Book House Co

Published by Baker Books
a division of Baker Book House Company

P.O. Box 6287, Grand Rapids, Michigan 49516-6287
Printed in the United States of America

Library of Congress Cataloging-in-Publication Data

Butcher, Debbie.
    Precious Moments Children's Bible Dictionary/ text by Debbie
Butcher; illustrations by Samuel J. Butcher.
       p.   cm.
   ISBN 0-8010-9736-3
   1. Bible—Dictionaries, Juvenile. I. Butcher, Samuel J. (Samuel
John), 1939– . III. Title.
BS440.W416   1994
220.3—dc20   94–19603

To
all the
precious
children in
the world

Debbie Butcher

As you use this dictionary

Young children are fascinated by language because learning it is one of their chief occupations. "What's that?" and "Why?" are questions preschoolers ask often as they are read to or told stories. Beginning and early readers have printed words and their meanings to add to their curiosity. The *Precious Moments Children's Bible Dictionary* is for children of these ages.

Children who hear or read Bible stories are blessed indeed, but the Bible presents them with an additional set of words to learn. Some words are unique to the Bible because it is about a different time, place, and culture. Some Bible words are familiar to Christians but are not part of the everyday vocabulary. Other words in the Bible have modern meanings that are different from the meaning in Bible times. Most of the words in this book fit one of these categories.

A dictionary for children cannot be complete or exhaustive. The entry words in this book were selected from the best-known stories in the Bible, rather than from its teachings, poems, or prophecies. We began by choosing words from *Precious Moments Stories from the Bible* and then surveyed stories commonly told to young children but not included in that book. A check of several other word lists provided the remaining key Bible story words.

Most of these words (except Trinity) appear in the New International Version of the Bible, and other English versions of the Bible. The "hard" words in the definitions have their own entries.

A dictionary is for browsing, which is the way most young children will use it by themselves. Adults who read Bible stories to them can help them look up the key words. The adults may learn a few new things too. We all smile over the misperceptions of Bible words we had as children. Finally, older children love to read to younger ones and be their teacher. If you can encourage an older child to read Bible stories to a younger one and teach the use of the dictionary, all kinds of blessings may come to both of them.

The Publisher

Aa

altar
Built like a platform or table, made of stones or metal. On altars things like meat or grain were burned as offerings or sacrifices to gods.

amen
A word to end a prayer that tells God our prayer is honest and we will accept the way he answers it; means "so be it."

angel
A being who does special work for God, such as bringing God's messages or taking care of people. Angels usually cannot be seen, but sometimes they do look like people, as when an angel appeared to Mary, the mother of Jesus, or to Peter and John as they stood in front of the empty tomb after Jesus arose. Artists often draw pictures of angels to look like people with wings.

anoint
To pour oil on a person, usually on the head, for one of four reasons: To make hair look better and smell good, or to make the head feel good. To be courteous to a guest. To use the oil as a medicine on a sore. To show that a person is chosen by God to be a prophet or a priest or a king.

altar

angel

Aa

apostle

One of the twelve special men Jesus chose to be near to him, to see him after his resurrection, and to begin to spread his message and start Christianity. Also called the twelve disciples.

ark

(1) A box-like boat, such as Noah's ark. (2) A covered box or chest, such as the Ark of the Covenant—the gold-covered chest in the Israelites' tabernacle that helped them know God was with them.

army

A group of people (always men in Bible times) who have weapons and are trained to fight battles or wars for their leader or their country.

armor

Hard, heavy clothing worn by soldiers for protection, made of metal, leather, or wood.

armor

The Twelve Apostles of Jesus

Andrew	The first apostle Jesus told to follow him; a fisherman; a leader of the twelve.
(Simon) Peter	Andrew's brother; a fisherman; one of the three disciples closest to Jesus.
James (Son of Zebedee)	Maybe Jesus' cousin; a fisherman; one of the three disciples closest to Jesus.
John	Brother of James; a fisherman; one of the three apostles closest to Jesus; wrote the Gospel According to John in the New Testament as well as three epistles and the Book of Revelation.
Philip	From the city of Bethsaida like Andrew and Peter.
Nathanael (Bartholomew)	Also from Bethsaida.
Matthew	A former tax collector (the kind hated by the Jews); wrote the Gospel According to Matthew in the New Testament.
Thomas	Also known as "the twin."
James (Son of Alphaeus)	Possibly Matthew's brother.
Simon	Also known as "the Zealot" because of the group he belonged to before he met Jesus.
Judas	Also called Thaddaeus; the least known of the twelve.
Judas Iscariot	The only one of the twelve who turned against Jesus, he betrayed Jesus to those who had him crucified.

Paul was not one of Jesus' twelve disciples, but he is also called an apostle because he saw Jesus after his resurrection and because Paul was the main person who spread the message about Jesus and started Christian churches.

Baal

A well-known heathen god (and smaller gods) of the Canaanite peoples in the Old Testament. Worshipers did some horrible things to try to please the Baal. The female Baal was Asherah.

baptize

To sprinkle water over a person or dip a person into water to show that the person believes Jesus has forgiven or washed away sins. The person's baptism means the Holy Spirit will help the person remember Jesus' great work.

bear

(1) A bear of Bible times was a yellowish-brown animal. (2) To bear something means to carry it, as to bear a problem or a gift; to give birth, or to bear a child; or to tell something, as to bear good news.

bear

baptize

beggar

A very poor person with no regular way to earn money who went into the streets to ask people for food or money.

believe

To know something is true; to trust someone or something. A *believer* is a person who believes in, or trusts, God and Jesus and what the Bible says. A *belief* is the idea or fact a person believes.

betray

(1) To turn against a person or people who trust or need us. (2) To help an enemy get ahold of a person or people who trust or need us.

birthright

The oldest son's double amount of his father's property when the father died, and that son's right to then be head of the family or tribe.

bless

(1) To help a person have good things and be happy. (2) To ask God to help another person have good things and be happy. (3) To tell God we think he is great and to thank him for good things. *A blessing* is a favor or a promise or a happiness from someone else or from God.

blind

(1) Not able to see well or not able to see anything with the eyes. (2) Not able to understand what God wants us to know.

blood

The red fluid that keeps the body alive. In the Bible, blood is a symbol, or reminder, of life.

bow

To bend the head forward, to bend the body forward, or to bend the knee. People bowed when they met, as when we say, "Hello, how are you?" or shake hands. To bow also shows respect for people and reverence for God.

bless

calf
A young bull or cow, a valuable animal used in some sacrifices.

camel
A large desert animal whose hooves (feet) are shaped to walk on sand, whose stomach stores extra water, and whose hump stores extra food. One kind of camel has one hump, the other has two humps.

Canaan
The land west of the Jordan River into which the Israelites moved after leaving Egypt and living in the wilderness. Also called Palestine and the Promised Land; *Canaanites* were the tribes of Canaan who were enemies of the Israelites for many years.

captive
(1) A person in prison. (2) In Bible times a person or group of people taken from their land and made to be slaves in an enemy's land.

carpenter
Person who builds things of wood such as buildings, furniture, and carts.

camel

carpenter

cart

Wooden wagon with usually two wooden wheels pulled by cows or oxen to carry people or grain or other things.

cattle

Bible word for farm and work animals such as camels, horses, sheep, goats, oxen, and donkeys.

cave

Opening in the side of a hill or cliff which may be tiny or may have many large rooms.

cedar

An evergreen tree whose very strong wood was used to make large or important buildings, pillars, ships, masts, and carvings.

celebrate

To do certain things, often in a particular way, with a group of people to honor or remember a good or happy event. A *celebration* can be a holiday or a party or a special church service.

chariot

A two-wheeled cart, sometimes made of iron and open in back, so that the rider or soldiers could stand in it while it was pulled by a horse. Used mostly in wars.

child

A son or daughter, young or old, who belonged to a family or tribe, or nation. The *children of Israel,* often called *Israelites,* were the descendants of Jacob (whose name was changed to Israel).

Christian

A follower of Jesus Christ or a member of his church.

church

(1) A building, sometimes called the Lord's house, where Christian people come together to worship God. (2) All the people in the world who are now Christians and all the people who ever were Christians.

church

clean

In Israel a clean person was free from disease or forgiven for a sin; a clean animal was a kind allowed to be used for food or as a sacrifice to God.

corn

The Bible word for all the grains, or cereal crops, and sometimes for all the vegetables together. Corn such as we have from the cob was not known in Bible times.

covenant

A promise or an agreement between two or more persons; a promise or an agreement between God and one or more persons.

create

To make something new that did not exist before; to bring it into being.

creation

The creation—God's creation—is the whole universe, which the Bible calls the heavens and the earth.

crops

Farm plants such as grains and fruits and vegetables that are raised for the growers to eat or to sell.

cross

Used in Jesus' time for the punishment of death, made of two pieces of wood fastened together in the shape of a "T." The person being put to death was usually nailed to the cross.

crowd

Many people gathered close together in a large group.

crown

A circle or cap, usually of gold, to show the person wearing it was a king, queen, high priest, or winner of a contest or battle.

crucify

To punish a criminal by nailing or hanging on a cross. The *crucifixion* of Jesus was his death on the cross as the punishment for all people's sins against God, even though Jesus had broken no laws.

cross

debt

(1) What someone has borrowed from someone else, usually money, that has to be paid back. (2) Something wrong done to someone else that has to be made right or punished.

den

A hollowed-out place like a cave where certain animals—lions, foxes, and bears—live.

desert

A very dry land; a place where plants, animals, and people can hardly live because of poor soil and little water; also called a *wilderness* in the Bible.

devil

A bad or evil spirit. The devil we usually think of is named *Satan*, the great enemy of God who tries to get people to sin. Evil spirits ruled by Satan are also called *demons*.

disciple

A student or a follower of a famous teacher. Jesus' disciples were all the people he taught who believed in him, but twelve disciples, called apostles, were especially close to him. (See also the word *apostle*.)

disease

(1) A sickness. (2) Something that is not right, is troublesome to a person's body or mind or soul, and may last a long time.

donkey

A small horselike animal used to plow fields, carry loads, pull carts, and carry people; also called an *ass* in the Bible. Kings rode donkeys to show they would work for the good of their people.

dove

A small, timid, gentle bird in the wild that could also be a loving pet; sometimes called a pigeon. Doves were used as sacrifices in the temple, and the dove is often used as a symbol of the Holy Spirit.

donkey

Ee

earth
(1) The world or planet we live on. (2) The land, not the sky or heavens or water.

Egypt
One of the oldest great nations of the world; the greatest nation during the time of the first part of the Old Testament. Egyptians were the people of Egypt.

enemy
(1) A person or group of people who work against or fight against another person or group of people. (2) Something dangerous like a disease or sin. (3) Another word for Satan (God's enemy).

epistle
A book or letter, such as the epistles Paul wrote to new Christian churches.

eternal
Never ending, such as eternal life with God; another word for everlasting.

evil
Sinful, wicked, harmful, horrible.

elder
(1) In the Old Testament, a prince or the head of a tribe, usually an older man, who was also in a group of rulers. (2) In the New Testament, a man who was one of the officers of each church who either taught or helped the church people.

Egypt

Earth

faith

Trust in a person, in God and Jesus, in a promise, or in an idea; hope; belief.

family

(1) All the children, parents, grandparents, and other relatives. (2) Relatives who live together. (3) A Bible word for all of the descendants of one person. (4) A group of people who love and care for each other. Christians are in God's family.

fast

To go without food and maybe water for a day or longer. People fasted to show they were very sad, or were very sorry they had sinned, or to show God they had a very special prayer request.

father

A Bible word for the man who began (was the ancestor of) a family or tribe or nation.

Father

When the word begins with a capital letter it is a name for God—God, the Father of all things. God the Father is the first person of the Trinity.

family

faith

feast

(1) A large delicious meal for many people who celebrate or have a joyful time. (2) A special religious or church meal at a certain time of the year, such as Passover; also called a *festival* in the Bible.

fig

A fruit grown on a tree, an important food to people in the Bible; also, a symbol, or reminder of God's goodness.

flock

A group of animals, such as sheep or birds, that stay together or are kept together.

flood

Too much water that has gathered into one place and overflowed to cover dry land.

fold

An enclosed place to keep sheep from wandering off and to protect them from thieves and wild animals; could be a fenced area or a cave.

forever

Without end.

forgive

(1) To give up hurt feelings or anger at someone who has done something against us. (2) To tell a person who owes us something that it does not have to be paid or returned.

frankincense and myrrh

(1) Frankincense was a good-smelling oil from a tree and was burned as part of offerings. (2) Myrrh was an oil from a tree. It had a perfume-like smell and was used to anoint people. If it was mixed with wine, could be used as a painkiller. Both were gifts from the wise men to Jesus.

furnace

A large oven about ten feet tall in which a very hot fire smelted iron ore (certain kind of rock) to make iron.

feast

Gg

gate
(1) Opening in a large wall, such as the wall of a city or castle or temple, through which people, carts, and animals and carts could come and go. (2) The door that closes an opening in a wall, often made of heavy wood or iron.

gentiles
People who were not of the Jewish nation or religion; today, Christians.

giant
A person much taller and bigger than most people and often stronger.

glory
(1) The praise, honor, or worship of someone great such as God. (2) Someone's power, importance, perfection, or great beauty; a good reason for much pride.

grace
(1) The love and protection God gives to people as a favor or free gift. (2) A short prayer before or after a meal.

god
Any object or person that people might worship.

gate

giant

God

The holy person who is a spirit we cannot see, who created the universe and earth and every living thing, who controls the universe, who is everywhere and lives within each of us, who loves and cares for us now and forever, who forgives our sins, who is perfect and fair and beautiful, and whom we love and praise and serve.

gospel

(1) The word that is not capitalized (gospel) means good news. The good news is that God loves us, which is the main thing Jesus taught and what pastors and missionaries preach. (2) The word that begins with a capital "G" (Gospel) means each of the first four books of the New Testament, which tell the story of Jesus' life.

governor

A person who ruled a country or part of a country because a higher ruler such as a king or emperor had put him in charge.

grave

A place in the ground where dead bodies are buried. In Bible times most graves were either natural or dug-out caves.

Greeks

(1) People who ruled the world before the Romans who were ruling in Jesus' time. (2) In the New Testament the word could mean any of the gentiles, especially educated ones, living in Palestine.

guard

A person, such as a soldier, who protected a ruler or whom the ruler might send to watch over a certain person or building or valuable things.

Other Names of God

Almighty **The Almighty**	All power and life are in God and from God and will be his forever.
God the Father	The name we use when we speak of God as the all-knowing creator and ruler of the universe and of all life.
God the Son	God became a person on earth when he was Jesus, whose mother was Mary.
God the Holy Spirit	The loving God lives in our hearts to teach, guide, and comfort us.
Jehovah	From the Hebrew name *Yahweh*, which means the God of grace (love) who shows himself to his people and is to be worshiped by them; God's most sacred name for himself.
Lᴏʀᴅ	The English word for the word the Old Testament writers used in place of *Yahweh*; means Master.

hallelujah
Said to mean "I praise the Lord" or to invite other people to praise the Lord.

harp
A musical instrument that was held on one arm and played with the fingers of the other hand plucking the strings.

harvest
To gather the ripe food crops, such as to pick grain or fruit or nuts.

hate
(1) To dislike or be angry about someone or something in the worst possible way. (2) *Hatred* is the opposite of love.

heal
To make a sickness go away; to make an injured or sore part of a body good again; to make a person well.

heart
The Bible word for the inside part of us that knows right from wrong, that loves, that is interested in things, that cares about things and people.

harp

heal

heaven

(1) A real place we cannot see but which is wonderful because it is filled with God's love and beauty, with angels, and with the souls of all of God's people; a place of more joy than we can imagine. (2) The Bible word for the whole universe.

Hebrews

People who spoke the Hebrew language; mainly, another name for Israelites.

hell

A place that cannot be seen but is horrible because God is not there and it has no love; a place of terrible punishment for Satan and his wicked angels and for people who do not follow God.

herd

A group of animals, such as cattle or horses, that stay together or are kept together.

holy

(1) Good, pure, perfect, wonderful, separate, and above everything else. God is holy. (2) Set apart for special use to worship God, such as the holy temple.

Holy Spirit

The Spirit of God; the power of God that comes into a person and teaches and helps that person to do something good and wonderful; also called Holy Ghost. God the Holy Spirit is the third person of the Trinity.

horn

Musical instrument that the player blows, made of the horn from an animal's head, or of metal.

humble

Not proud; plain, ordinary; not seeming to be important.

hymn

A song to praise God.

hymn

idol

(1) A thing (not God) that people worship or admire very much. (2) Something people have made of metal or stone or wood—usually in the shape of a person or animal—to worship as a god.

image

(1) A copy or reflection of something else. People are copies or reflections of God—made in his image. (2) Another word for idol.

inn

In Bible times a walled shelter or group of wooden stalls where travelers could spread their mats and sleep, store their goods, keep their cattle, and get water.

island

A piece of land with water all around it. An island can be very small or large enough to have cities and farms, forests and mountains.

Israel

(1) A man named Jacob who was also named Israel. (2) The nation whose people had all descended form Jacob (Israel).

Israelites

All people descended from Jacob (whose name was also Israel), who spoke the Hebrew language, who made up the nation of Israel, and who were chosen by God to be the first to receive his promises.

inn

A city in **Israel**

jealousy

A terrible feeling against someone who has something better than we have.

Jesus

The name means Jehovah is salvation. Before Jesus was born the angel told Mary his mother that Jesus would save his people from their sins.

Jews

(1) People of the tribe of Judah or the kingdom of Judah in the Old Testament. (2) Hebrews and all Israelites who lived in Palestine or anywhere in the world. (3) People of today who are descended from the Israelites or who follow the Jewish laws and customs.

journey

A trip; travel from one place to another.

judge

(1) A person who knows the laws and decides if someone with a problem is right or wrong. (2) In the Old Testament, a person who led the people to defeat the enemy and then made sure there was peace.

journey

Other Names of Jesus

Christ	From the Greek word that means *anointed one:* Jesus was chosen (anointed) by God the Father to be the only Savior.
Lamb of God	Jesus was a sacrifice—from God to God—for the sins of other people, like the real lambs in Old Testament sacrifices.
Lord	A ruler or master: Jesus is Lord of our hearts; also, a polite word like *Sir* said by people in Bible times.
Master	The best teacher; ruler; Sir.
Messiah	From the Hebrew word that means anointed one: Jesus was the great king God had promised the people of the Old Testament.
Rabbi	The Hebrew word for teacher.
Savior	The one who saves, or rescues, us from the dangers of sin and hell.
Son **Son of God**	God was Jesus' Father and Mary was his mother. God the Son is the second person of the Trinity.
Son of Man	Jesus was a human being, or man, as well as God.

Kk

king

The head ruler or most powerful ruler over a group of people such as one tribe or one city, but usually over a whole country.

kingdom

(1) The group of people or the land ruled over by a king. (2) The kingdom of God, also called the kingdom of heaven, can mean the whole universe, or it can mean all the people who ever allowed God to rule their hearts and souls.

kiss

(1) In Bible times a greeting, such as our handshakes, between two men, between two women, between relatives and friends, or between people very happy to see each other. (2) In Bible times to kiss a king's feet showed great respect for him and his work.

know

(1) To have all the information about something. (2) To understand something very well, often through being close to or experiencing it. (3) *Knowledge* is what we know.

kiss

king

Ll

lamb
A young sheep, often used for sacrifice. Jesus was called the Lamb of God because he was sacrificed for our sins.

lame
Having weak or sore or stiff arms or legs; not able to walk normally; crippled.

land
(1) The dry part of the earth, separate from water and air.

(2) A certain large place that a group of people owned and live on, also called a country.

law
(1) A rule or set of rules about how to act or live. (2) The first five books of the Old Testament. (3) The set of rules God gave to Moses, often called the Ten Commandments.

leper
A person who had leprosy which, because the Jewish law called it unclean, made the person live separately from everyone else and shout, "Unclean" if anyone came near.

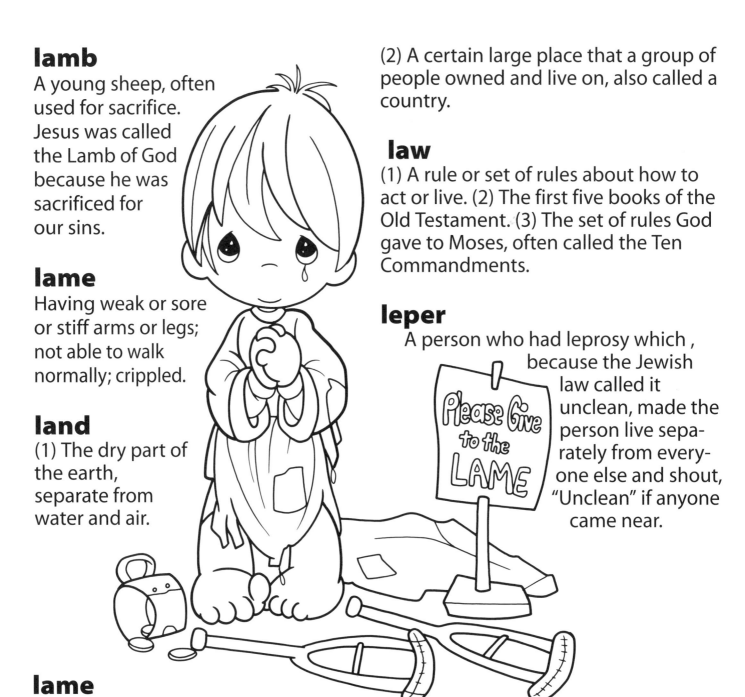

Please Give to the LAME

lame

lamb

leprosy
(1) The disease in Bible times that made bad sores on the skin and caused the hair by the sores to turn white. It could last for many years but could also disappear by itself. (2) The modern disease of the same name that causes fingers, toes, arms, and legs to become numb. Lepers can badly injure themselves without feeling it.

Levite
A man born into the tribe of Levi, who was to be a worker in the tabernacle or temple as helper to the priests, caretaker of the building and its furnishings, musician, writer, or judge.

locust
An insect something like a grasshopper which, if there were too many, destroyed crops. Locusts were clean insects and could be roasted or sun dried and salted for food.

Lord's Supper
Also called the Last Supper or communion, in which Christian churches remember the last meal Jesus and his twelve disciples had together before he died. Christians think about what Jesus said, and that he loved us so much he gave his life for us.

lots
To help make choices or decisions, the people prayed and then put into a container two stones with writing on them, shook the container, and emptied it. The way the stones landed gave the answer.

love
(1) To care for someone very much and to value that person. (2) To want to do the very best thing we can for someone else and actually to do it, even if it's better for that person than for us.

love

man

(1) The Bible word for all people or humans—women and men, girls and boys. (2) Can also mean a man, as Adam was the first man.

meek

manger

A box to hold food for cattle; in Bible times usually made of small stones and mortar (material that holds the stones together); could also be a hollowed-out section of a cave wall. It was not often made of wood.

manna

The food God provided for the Israelites in the wilderness after they left Egypt for the Promised Land, which looked like white seeds that covered the ground; also called bread from heaven.

market

The busy place in the city where farmers sold food and merchants sold goods, outdoors or in stalls.

meek

Not bossy or trying to be the most important; gentle, kind, not wanting to quarrel.

manger

marriage

The time when a man and woman, who love each other and have promised to take care of each other all their lives, leave their separate homes and live together as husband and wife. Usually there is a feast or party to celebrate this happy time.

message

An idea or information or instruction that is delivered in a speech or a writing. The message of the Bible is that God loves us through Jesus Christ.

minister

In the Old Testament a person who served or took care of the person he worked for; in the New Testament the servant of the church's people. All Christians are ministers to each other, to Jesus, and to all people.

miracle

Something that God makes happen that does not happen in ordinary ways; a sign of what God is and can do.

money

(1) In early times not used much, people traded things instead; in the New Testament the Roman's silver coins are mentioned. (2) A person's wealth was measured by the amount of land, animals, and crops he had.

messenger

marriage

nation

(1) A large amount of land with borders and one government; a country.
(2) A group of people, larger than a tribe, from one ancestor or "father."

New Testament

The last twenty-seven books of the Bible. The New Testament tells about Jesus' life and the beginnings of Christianity, has Paul's letters to the new churches, and has the Book of Revelation about the end times.

noble

A man whose family had been rulers or rich for many years and so he was a ruler also.

Old Testament
New Testament

Oo

obey

To do what God tells us to do through the Bible, or through his people who have a right to tell us what to do, or through what we know and understand we should do.

offer

To give something to God or the church as an act of worship, a sign of love for God; to sacrifice. The *offering* is the thing that is given.

oil

A liquid collected or pressed from olives and used for burning in lamps, in baking bread, as medicine, to anoint kings and priests, and to soothe the body and smooth the hair.

Old Testament

The first thirty-nine books of the Bible. The Old Testament tells about the beginning of the world and the story of the Israelites until about six hundred years before Jesus. It also has books of poetry and prophecies.

ox

An animal larger than a cow but similar, used for plowing, for pulling wagons, or as a sacrifice.

palm
A tall straight tree with no branches but with huge leaves at the tip that are sometimes called branches; its fruit is dates; it grows in Bible lands and other warm places.

parable
A saying or a short story to help people understand an idea or a lesson.

Passover
The religious festival of the Jews to celebrate being freed from slavery in Egypt, especially the night the Lord passed over the Israelites' houses sprinkled with lambs' blood but killed all the firstborn Egyptians; also called the feast of unleavened bread.

Pentecost
A Jewish harvest festival called the feast of weeks held seven weeks after Passover. On the well-known New Testament Pentecost seven weeks after Easter, the Holy Spirit came to the first Christians. That was the beginning of the Christian church.

persecute
To be unfair and very mean to a person or group of persons, maybe over a long period of time, because they look or believe a certain way.

pharaoh
An Egyptian king. There were many famous pharaohs in the Bible.

Pharisees
A small group of religious leaders who followed strict Jewish rules and made up new ones, who usually thought they were better than other people, who were not kind, who did not understand forgiveness, and who therefore hated Jesus because he was opposite from them.

palm

Philistines

People of Canaan who were especially strong enemies of the Israelites from the time of Joshua to King David in the Old Testament.

plague

(1) A disease that many people have at the same time. A bad happening that can cause much destruction or many deaths. In the Old Testament God used plagues to punish groups of people for their sins.

poor

Not having enough of what is necessary. Poor people may not have enough food or good clothes or enough money for good houses.

pray

To talk to God to tell him we love him, to thank him, and to ask him for ordinary and special things we and other people need. Prayer is often spoken to the Father in Jesus' name.

pray

Plagues on Egypt

God sent a plague on the Egyptians each time the pharaoh refused to let the Israelites leave Egypt to be led by Moses. There were ten plagues in all, and after the last one the pharaoh sent the Israelites away. None of the plagues touched the Israelites.

1   River water changed into blood.

2.   The land was overrun by frogs.

3.   Lice, or gnats, came from the dust and covered all the people and animals.

4.   Swarms of flies ruined all kinds of things.

5.   All the farm animals got sick and died.

6.   The people and animals were covered with such bad sores called boils. They were too sick to stand up.

7.   Large hailstones in a terrible storm killed people and animals who were outside and destroyed all the ripe crops in the fields.

8.   Clouds of locusts ate every green thing still left after the hail.

9.   It was so dark for three days and nights people could not see each other or leave their houses.

10.   Every firstborn male of the people and animals died.

priest

A person like a minister who works in a temple or a church to bring the people and God together; the person who does the acts of sacrifice at the altar. In Bible times all nations had priests in the worship of their gods.

prison

A place to keep people who broke certain laws, who were accused of breaking certain laws, or sometimes to keep them from breaking laws; also a place to keep captured enemies; a jail, but in Bible times not special buildings like our jails.

promise

(1) What a person says he or she will do for sure, usually for another person. (2) The thing that someone promised comes true.

Promised Land

The land that God promised Abraham and the Israelites would be theirs; Canaan, also called Palestine.

prophet

A person who talks with God or tells God's messages to the people. To prophesy is to receive and then tell the message. In Bible times the message from God, also called a prophecy, would be either a promise of good things or a prediction of bad things such as punishments.

proud

Pleased with ourselves or with what we have done. To be proud of what is truly fine or of what we have done well is good, if we remember that God has helped us. But to be so proud we try to make someone else feel badly is the opposite of Christian love.

proverb

A short saying that tells something wise or true and is easy to remember. The Book of Proverbs is in the Old Testament.

prophet

Pp

psalm
A poem or song that praises God or tells about praising God. The Book of Psalms is in the Old Testament.

publican
Men in Jesus' time who collected tax money from the Jews for the ruling Romans and who dishonestly charged people too much and then kept the extra for themselves. The Jews hated not only the Romans but also the Jews who were publicans.

punish
To make a person pay a price for breaking a law. Punishment is the payment for being guilty.

He that is without sin among you Let him cast the First Stone

punish

quail
A small brown bird like a partridge. God sent quails for food to the Israelites when they were in the wilderness after they left Egypt.

quarrel
A big argument or fight; to not get along with other people.

queen
(1) The wife of a king; the most important wife of a king who had more than one wife. (2) A woman who rules alone and is equal to a king.

quench
(1) To put out a fire. (2) To make sad or to discourage. (3) To give water or liquid to take away thirst.

queen

raise

To raise someone from the dead, which Jesus did, means to awaken or to lift the person from being dead to being alive again.

raven

A large black bird in the crow family.

repent

To change our minds about wanting to do wrong things, to be sorry about doing wrong things, to stop doing wrong things, and to do right things instead.

resurrection

The rising or coming back to life after being dead. The resurrection of Jesus was three days after he died on the cross, and we celebrate it on Easter.

robber

A person who robs or steals; a thief.

Romans

People of the Roman Empire, which ruled the world during Jesus' time.

ruler

(1) A person who is in charge or has power to decide what other people would do and makes them do it. (2) In Bible times a person who saw to it that the laws of the religion or of the city were obeyed.

resurrection

Ss

Sabbath
Day of rest set aside to honor God, that God told Moses was to be a holy day for the Israelites. To honor Jesus' resurrection on the first day of the week, Christians have Sunday as their Sabbath day.

sacrifice
Something given to God as a gift of praise or thanksgiving or as payment for sin; offering. Sacrifices were almost always burned on an altar, usually by a priest in the tabernacle or temple.

saint
In the Bible the word *saint* meant all people who belong to God, who love him. Today special Christians sometimes are called saints.

Samaritan
People who lived in a part of Palestine called Samaria and who were part Jewish. The Jews of Jesus' time thought they were better than the Samaritans and hated them.

save
To rescue from danger or evil; to be rescued from sin and its punishment.

Savior
Jesus; the rescuer. Jesus saved us from the dangers of our own sins when he took the punishment for our sins.

save

scribe

A man who copied written things by writing with a reed pen dipped in ink on papyrus (paper of that time) or leather scrolls—the only way to make copies since there were no printed books. Scribes also taught the laws.

Scripture

(1) All the Bible books of the Old Testament. (2) The sacred writings of the Jews (some are not in the Bible). (3) The law of Moses—the first five books of the Bible. (4) Today for Christians it means any part of the Bible.

sea

(1) The ocean, the largest body of water (salt water) on the earth. (2) A very large body of water but not as big as the ocean, either salt or fresh water. (3) A very large lake.

serpent

Snake; a snakelike creature.

servant

(1) A person who works for or takes care of other people. (2) A person who worships and works for God. (3) A Bible word for *slave.*

serve

(1) To help another person or people, either for pay or for no pay. (2) To love and respect another person and do what that person wants us to do.

shepherd

A person who takes care of sheep.

sin

(1) To do something bad—against what God wants or commands—or to refuse to do the right thing. (2) The action that is against what God wants or commands.

slave

A person owned by another person and forced to work for the owner.

shepherd

sling

A weapon for throwing a stone. It was made of a piece of leather that held a stone and was attached to two strings that were whirled around the head; one string was let go, and the stone flew out.

soldier

A man in the army. Some men were soldiers only when there was a war, some had lifetime jobs being soldiers.

soul

The spirit or invisible part of a person that will live forever after the body dies.

spear

A weapon made of a long pole with a sharp metal point on the end. It was to be thrown at an enemy animal or person, to hurt or kill.

swaddling clothes

A cloth that was wrapped around a new baby and fastened by strips of cloth wound around the outside.

sword

A long knife with one or two sharp edges carried in a sheath attached to a belt. It was used mostly by soldiers against enemies.

sycamore

A tree of Bible lands important for its figlike fruit and for the shade of its widespread branches (not the same as the North American sycamore).

synagogue

A building, something like a church, that each town had where the Jewish people listened to preaching, studied, and prayed.

soldier

tabernacle
The tent church Moses had built after the Israelites left Egypt and which was used until King Solomon built the temple at Jerusalem.

tablets of stone
Flat pieces of stone with writing that had been engraved, or cut, into both sides. On such stone God wrote the Ten Commandments for Moses (also called tables of stone).

tax
To make the people who belong to a city or nation pay the government a certain amount of money or goods. Taxes pay for the government and for the things people use, such as roads.

temple
A place of worship, often a large building. The temple at Jerusalem was the headquarters of the Jewish people's worship of God.

Ten Commandments
The main laws God gave to the Israelites through Moses, which we still use today.

Ten Commandments

10 Commandments	Meaning
1. You shall have no other gods before me.	Jehovah is the only true God there is to worship.
2. You shall not make for yourself an idol to worship.	God is the most important thing or person for us to love, even though we cannot see him.
3. You shall not misuse the name of the LORD your God.	God is so holy we must respect even his names.
4. Remember the Sabbath day by keeping it holy.	One day a week is for rest and special worship to God.
5. Honor your father and mother.	Love and obey your parents and help them when you can.
6. You shall not murder.	God made and loves every person and wants us to love and help each other, not hurt or kill each other.
7. You shall not commit adultery.	Married people promise always to try to love each other and to have sex only with each other.
8. You shall not steal.	Respect other people's property, and help poor people.
9. You shall not give false testimony against your neighbor.	Say only the truth about other people and nothing mean or troublesome.
10. You shall not covet.	Try not to be jealous of other people or their things, but be happy for them and satisfied with what you have.

(See Exodus 20 for complete wording.)

thorns

The Bible word for prickly, or spine-bearing, weeds, bushes, or small trees.

tower

A tall, narrow booth for watchmen of a vineyard or sheepfold; a tall, narrow building to hold soldiers guarding and defending a city at its gates and on its walls.

trial

A time when a person who is accused of breaking a law has to go to court. There a judge or a jury decides if the person is guilty and what the punishment will be.

Trinity

God the Father, God the Son, and God the Holy Spirit. (This word is not in the Bible.)

trust

A feeling of being sure that someone will take care of us or do what is good for us, or that something will work right; faith.

thorns

unbelief

No faith, or trust, in God's love; not believing God's promises or that he will keep them.

unleavened bread

Bread made without yeast, so it does not rise and become soft and airy. It stays flat and hard like a cracker.

unfaithful

(1) To break a promise. (2) Not living up to what we believe or know is right.

unrighteous

Unfair, wicked.

upbuilding

Making bigger or better.

uproar

A big noise made by a large group of people who are very excited, often angry.

veil

(1) A large curtain that divided the room in the tabernacle (and later the temple) called the Holy of Holies from the room called the Holy Place. (2) A long piece of cloth used by women in Bible times to cover their heads and shoulders and sometimes their faces.

vessel

Something, such as a cup or pot, that holds a liquid in it. Sometimes a boat is called a sailing vessel.

victory

The winning of a contest or a battle.

vine

A long, thin-stemmed plant such as a grapevine. A vineyard is a garden or farm of grapevines.

vision

A special kind of dream in which a person sees something that is greater than ordinary, such as an angel or a prophecy.

vow

(1) A promise to do an act or behave a certain way, sometimes using a sign to bind the promise. (2) To make such a promise.

vessel

wall

Most towns and cities of Bible times had houses and streets close together inside a thick wall that had gates and towers which surrounded the city. The gardens and farms were outside the wall.

war

Either one battle or many battles over many years between groups of people such as tribes or countries.

weapon

A tool that is used to attack someone or to defend against an enemy.

wheat

A grass crop whose seed, or grain, is ground into flour for bread and other foods.

weapon

wicked
Very bad; very mean; against God.

widow
A woman whose husband has died. In Bible times life was hard for widows because women did not go out to work for money.

wine
Grape juice that has been treated in a special way so that it will not spoil but will change to wine. It was served during celebrations and by Jesus at his Last Supper as a sign of life and love.

wise
Having knowledge and being able to use knowledge to make good choices or decisions.

world
(1) The earth; the planet we live on. (2) The earth or universe that is not the spiritual heaven. (3) The Bible word for the small part of the world known in Bible times. (4) A Bible word for people who did not serve God.

worship
To praise God, honor God, and tell or show him we really love him. We worship God in church, and we can worship him anytime and in any place.

world

worship

yarn
Thick thread made by spinning the fibers of the flax plant (woven into linen cloth) or of animal hair (woven into wool cloth).

year
Twelve months. The Hebrew new year began with the spring harvest (around our April). Summer was dry, and grain was planted in autumn.

yeast
Something added to bread dough to make it light and fluffy. Yeast is also used in making wine.

yoke
(1) A wooden bar to hold two oxen together at the necks so they will pull a cart or plow together. (2) A pair of oxen held together in that way.

youth
A young person; a teenager.

yield
(1) To give out naturally, such as a tree that will yield fruit. (2) To give in to someone or something that is stronger.

zeal
Excitement and willingness to work hard for something that is strongly believed in.

Zion
(1) One of the hills on which the city of Jerusalem was built. (2) The name given to the hill where the temple was built. (3) Another name for the whole city of Jerusalem. (4) The Jewish church. (5) A New Testament name for heaven.